Rapid Reading Series

Celine and Cyrus
Book 14

Written by G. Grafi
©2021

For the Graf Siblings.
With love.

A note to parents and teachers: This is the fourteenth book in the Rapid Reading series. Its purpose is to practice the soft "c" words.

Follow the guide and use the tables on the next page to practice the soft "c" words prior to reading the book in order to facilitate the reading process.

Sight words are high frequency words that often repeat themselves in many beginning books. Sight words are remembered rather than read. It is recommended to practice sight words as well.

Dr. G. Grafi

Here is the rule for reading the hard and soft "c":

When the "c" is followed by an "e", an "i" or a "y", the letter "c" makes the "s" sound.

All other letters that follow the "c", make the "k" sound.

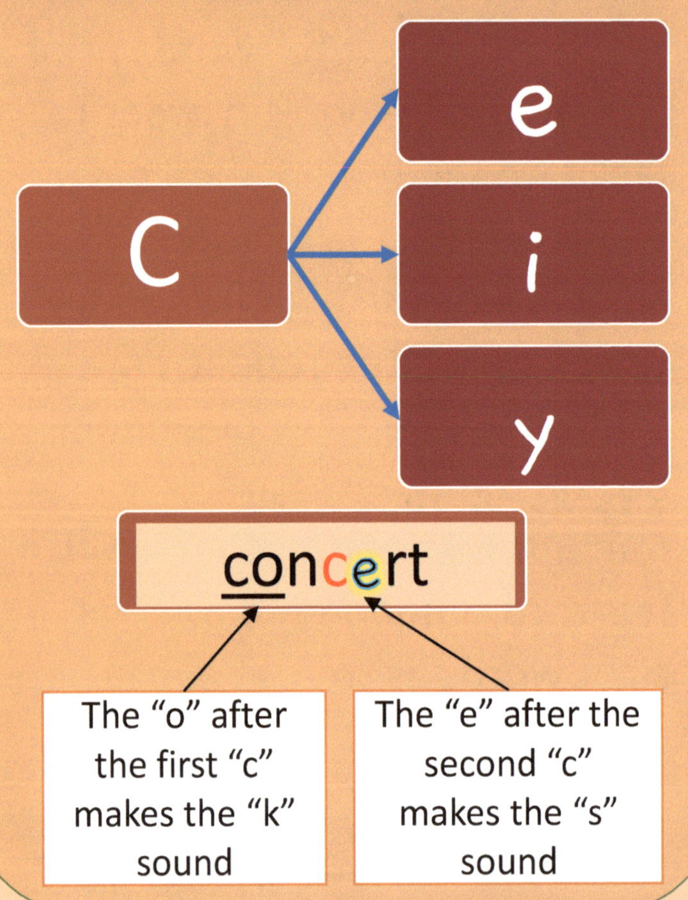

Soft "c" words in this book.

Celine	celery	fence
Cyrus	juice	police
city	cellar	space
center	cymbals	race
cereal	price	mice
cell	cycles	rice
face	bicycle	ice
circle	voice	spicy
dance	nice	circus
concert	pencil	

Sight Words in this book.

Doesn't	goes	uses
live	juice	some
talks	every	now
phone	also	ones
puts	people	who
wears	show	watch
earrings	many	
before	come	

This is Celine. Celine doesn't live in the city center.

In the morning, Celine eats cereal and talks on her cell phone.

Celine then puts makeup on her face and wears the circle earrings.

Celine can't wait to sing
and dance at the concert.

Before she goes to the concert, Celine makes a carrot and celery juice.

This is Cyrus.

Cyrus also doesn't live in
the city center.

Every morning, Cyrus goes to the cellar to play his cymbals and drums.

Cyrus also can't wait
to sing and dance at
the concert.

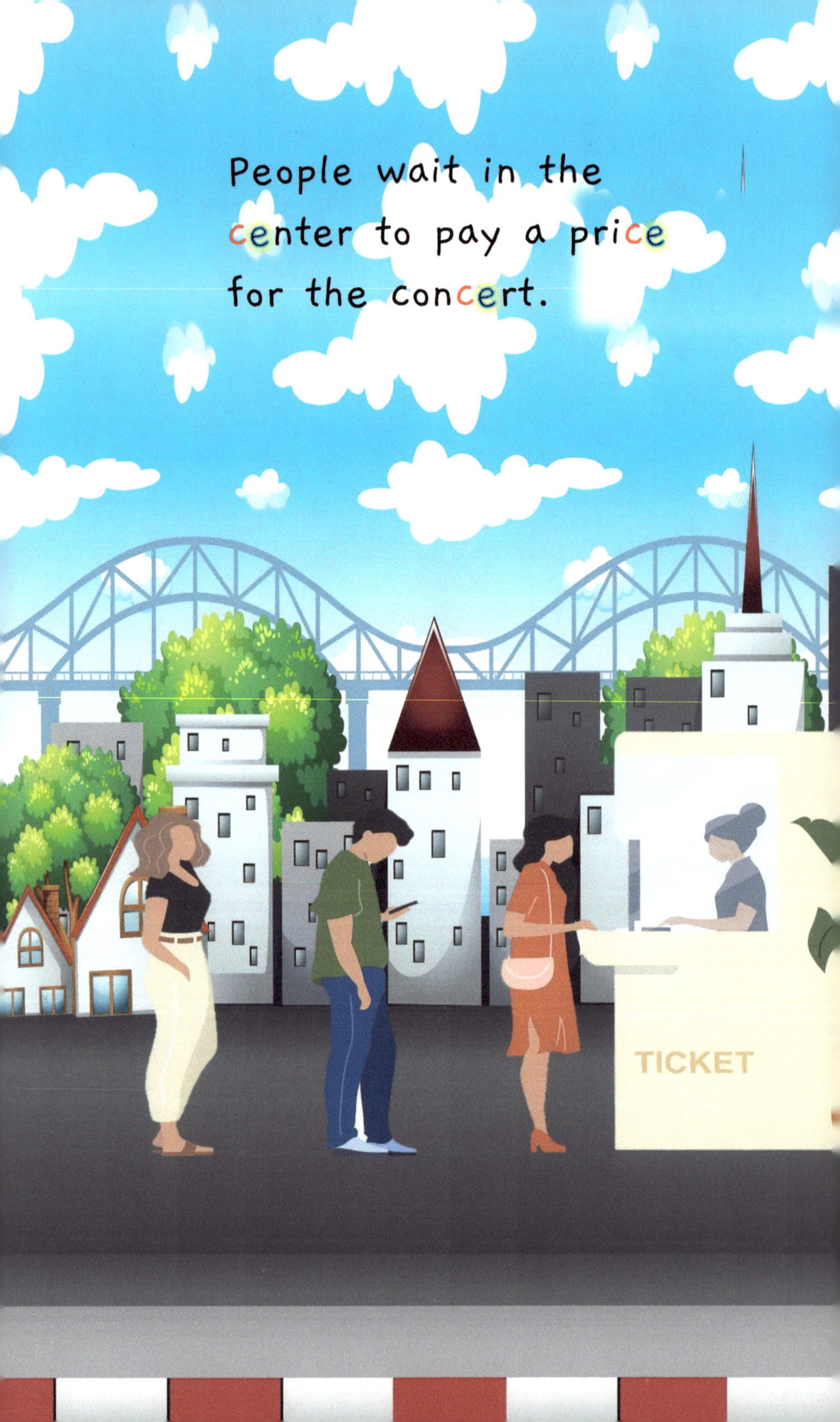

People wait in the center to pay a price for the concert.
TICKET

Celine goes to the city center to put on a show with Cyrus.

Cyrus cycles to the city center on his bicycle to put on a show with Celine.

Many people come to see the concert with Celine and Cyrus.

The people like Celine's voice
and they think she is nice.

After the concert, Cyrus
uses a pencil by the fence
and then leaves the city.

The police help clear
up the space after
the concert.

So that after the concert
Celine and Cyrus race like
mice to leave the show.

When Celine gets home, she eats some rice and then some ice cream.

When Cyrus gets home, he makes a spicy meal and lets his voice rest.

Now Celine and Cyrus go to the circus to be the ones who watch the stage.